CREDITS

Cover Design
Articulate Solutions ® Inc.

cover image courtesy
shutterstock.com

Photography and Content
Linda Estill

Book Design
Shannon Duarte

Other Photography
A.K. Rowland Photography

Published by
THE DO-IT-YOURSELF-FLORIST ENTERPRISES ™
2425 Olea Court, Gilroy, CA 95020
(408) 848-5234

ISBN: 978-0-9794595-1-1
EBook ISBN: 978-0-9794595-0-4

Flowers Made Simple

Remember how special and delighted you felt the last time you received a gorgeous bouquet of flowers? Imagine what it would be like if you could experience the thrill of giving that feeling to a friend or loved one without ever calling the florist! Visualize yourself presenting a fragrant basket or vase of spectacular, perfectly arranged flowers to your best friend. Picture the look of surprise and amazement on his or her face when you say, "I made it myself!" My name is Linda Estill and I'm a certified florist and event planner in the Bay Area of California. It's not my goal to turn you into a professional florist, nor can I teach you all there is to know about flowers. I want to share with you the magic and inspiration that I feel every time I gather nature's miracles and use them to create all sorts of innovative designs and floral arrangements. Believe me, as you work... actually PLAY with flowers and foliage, you will find yourself overcome with a sense of peace and serenity unlike anything you've ever experienced. Get ready to discover some of the secrets of the pros while you learn how to arrange flowers just for the fun of it!

To my dad who helped me plant my
first garden, and who taught me that
the path to inner peace can be found
among the wonders of nature.

ten tips

Do you wish your cut flowers would last longer? Follow these 10 tips to selecting the cream of the crop and extending the life of your beautiful arrangements.

tip 1. Make your selection from those flowers furthest from your reach. Flowers are rotated according to their age and you can be sure, the oldest ones will usually be the easiest to access.

tip 2. If flowers are displayed in tiered fashion and you have a choice, make your selection from the upper tiers. When you pull a bouquet from the bucket, notice how drops of water fall onto the lower bouquets. This causes mold and brown spots on those flowers. Try to avoid dripping on surrounding flowers as much as possible.

tip 3. Look for erect heads and stems. If a stem, head or tip of a flower, such as a gladiola, is drooping or bent, the flower is old or it can no longer draw water for various reasons.

tip 4. Look for perky petals. If you see wilted petals like those on this pink posy, or even worse, loose, fallen petals, avoid that bunch and move on.

tip 5. If the petals show signs of browning like these formerly white carnations, buyer beware.

tip 6. When buying roses, purchase those with the fewest cracked petals and the tightest heads. Gently squeeze the base of the head. You want those that feel firm and tight to the touch. Notice how the edges of these rose petals are dark, the insides are faded and they look very limp. Not a good choice. Also beware of brown mold spots.

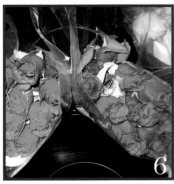

7 Yellowing leaves and stems are a sure sign that that bouquet is on its last legs. Another indication that death is imminent is slime. Watch for that on the stems. Also look for the freshest cut on the stems. A dark ring around the base means the cut is old and the flower hasn't been able to drink as much as it wants to.

8 Look for flowers with bright, vibrant colors. If the petals look faded, the flowers are dated.

9 Don't buy flowers such as lilies with loose pollen on the petals.

10 Once you've made your purchase, get it home as soon as possible and follow these guidelines:

a. If you're not going to arrange them right away, remove the wrapping, cut the string or rubber band and put the flowers into a clean sink or bucket of warm water (except chrysanthemums which prefer cool water). Warm water travels up the stem faster.

b. Arrange them in the container as soon as practical. Your vase or container should be squeaky clean. Bacteria is a flower's worst enemy!

c. Treat the water with the package of flower food usually contained in the bouquet or add a couple of drops of bleach and a half teaspoon of sugar. (Opinions are varied on sugar; some say it promotes bacteria growth). Flower food is your best bet.

d. Remove all leaves and foliage below the water's surface. They are another source of bacteria and they will make your arrangement stink!

e. Cut ALL stems at an angle before putting them into the vase. They will be able to drink more water and they'll love you for this.

f. Keep your finished arrangement in a cool location away from heat or drafts.

To extend the life of your masterpiece, give the stems a fresh cut each day, add fresh water, and make your flowers smile with a light mist from a spray bottle whenever you think of it. Be sure the mist is light; you don't want puddles in your petals.

The happier you make your flowers, the happier they'll make you!

5

supplies

Y ou don't need a lot of expensive supplies to arrange flowers, and you should be able to find everything at your local craft store or major discount department store. Also see if you have a floral supply center in your area, or look online.

Floral Scissors or Cutting Shears

Yes, professional florists use floral knives but that skill takes a little practice and I don't want you to bleed. Whatever you use, make sure it's clean. Flowers worst enemy is bacteria. It is a good idea to have a sharp knife on hand to remove leaves and thorns from stems.

Florist's or Bowl Tape

This is a waterproof tape specifically designed for floral work. You could also use cellophane, masking or other narrow tape, but bowl tape is your best bet. It comes in green or clear. Be careful not to get stem wrap.

Floral Foam

Get several blocks of this as we use it in a number of designs. Make sure to get the foam designed for fresh flowers, not artificial.

tips

There are a lot of other things you could get

- wire
-floral adhesive
-stem wrap

but it's not necessary to spend a lot of money when you're just starting out.

Keep it simple for now.

Containers

You can start with some simple vases, the likes of which you probably have under your kitchen sink. And start saving your recyclables, frozen food trays, styrofoam trays, deli containers and even two liter soda bottles.

designing using *layers*

One secret to creating beautiful vased arrangements is the use of layers. By following this simple guide, your bouquets will look so professional, you'll even amaze yourself!

INITIAL LINE FOLIAGE

1 Start by making a grid across the top of your vase with florist's or cellophane tape and create a triangle with your line foliage. This could be leather leaf or sword fern, huckleberry, ruscus...linear type greens.

2 Add a few more stems of line foliage all around the vase. Always point your materials toward an imaginary X in the center of the container.

REMAINDER LINE FOLIAGE

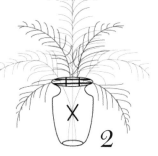

3 Then add some round foliage, like salal, camellia, eucalyptus, ivy, pitisporum, etc. Round foliage has more bulk than line foliage and helps to create a "nest" for your flowers.

ROUND FOLIAGE

LINE FLOWERS

Some types include: hybrid tea rose buds, snapdragons, larkspur or delphinium, gladiola, liatris, bells of Ireland, tuberose, or calla lilies.

4 Line Flowers are long and tapered and, along with your foliage, they help to define the overall shape of your arrangement.

MASS FLOWERS

5

5 Mass Flowers are smaller than the focal flowers, although, depending on your design, they could be considered your focal flower.

Some types include: roses, smaller mums, carnations, lisianthus, iris, daffodils, daisies, ranunculus, anemones, miniature gerberas, stock, viburnum.

7 Filler Material is not always needed, but usually used to provide additional texture or airy-ness.

6 Focal Flowers are large, "roundish" flowers that immediately catch your attention in an arrangement.

FOCAL FLOWERS

6

Some types include: hydrangea, sunflowers, lilies, cabbage roses, gerbera daisies, peonies, dahlias, zinnias, spider or large pom, pom chrysanthemums, anthurium, protea, amaryllis and several others. *Think Big!*

FILLER MATERIAL

7

Some types include: baby's breath, misty blue (limonium), solidaster, wax flower, teaberry, alstromeria, Queen Anne's lace, rice flower, statice, or safflower. Even pods and grasses.

tips

-Add floral food or a teaspoon of bleach and a little sugar to your vase.

-Remove all leaves below the water's surface.

-Cut stems at an angle.

-Turn your vase as you work, filling in gaps as you go.

country charm

You can use all sorts of flowers to create a spectacular vased arrangement like this one.

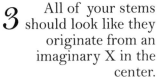

1 Take your vase (flared vases work best) and using your florist's or cellophane tape (see "Supplies"), make a grid across the top, which acts as a support structure for your materials.

2 Your first stem of line foliage should be about one and a half times the height of your vase and placed into the center of your grid. The next two stems should be slightly shorter and inserted on either side of your first stem to create a triangle.

3 All of your stems should look like they originate from an imaginary X in the center.

4 Next add your round foliage; here I've used camellia. Spraying foliage with leaf shine really helps to make your arrangement look even more professional.

5 Insert your line flowers almost like you did your line foliage. I've used three stems of luscious purple larkspur.

6 Next I've added three stems of white stock. Of course you could use almost any color.

7 Add your mass flowers all around your design, cutting them to different lengths, but do not go outside the triangle. I've used three lilac scabiosa and one stem of white daisy mum.

8 Turn your vase and fill in the gaps. I've included a few golden dahlias, but you could use whatever you want, even use just one type, such as roses. There are so many types of mass flowers, your choice is almost unlimited.

9 Notice how the brilliant orange sunflowers capture your immediate attention. A few have been placed more toward the base of the design. You could also use sunny, gerbera daisies.

10 Just a few stems of yellow solidaster inserted throughout the arrangement give it the almost-final touch. Think of what other types of filler you could use.

tips

-cut the stems at an angle for more water absorption.

-put your floral materials in a bucket or sink of room temperature water that's been treated with flower food or a teaspoon or two of chlorine bleach and a teaspoon of sugar.

11 A small, inexpensive remnant of burlap secured with a rubber band covers the stems and gives the bouquet an added touch of country charm! You may even want to tie it with a few strands of raffia. Other types of fabric could also be used. Use your imagination!

grocery store to vase

Now that you've learned how to buy flowers, the basics of flower arranging and how to design using layers, let's work with a mixed bouquet that can be purchased at almost any grocery or discount department store. You don't want to just plop it into a vase as is, do you? The answer, of course, is "no".

1 Separate your foliage and flowers by types. Remove the lower leaves – remember, no leaves below the water's surface.

2 Fill your clean vase with water and add the package of flower food that most likely came with the bouquet. Tape a grid across the top using waterproof florist's tape or cellophane tape.

3 Begin with your greens, pointing them toward an imaginary X in the center and filling all around. If your bouquet doesn't have many, consider adding some from your yard.

By following these simple steps, you can transform any store-bought bouquet into a beautiful, professional looking arrangement that will brighten up your home or workplace!

4 Determine what you're going to use as your line flower. The best choice with this bouquet is the solidaster, although it's sometimes used as filler. Notice how it creates a triangle.

5 Continue with your mass flowers. You'll want to separate flowers like chrysanthemums, carnations and statice from the main stem. This gives you more flowers to work with.

7 Add your focal flowers, such as the gerbera daisies and sunflowers in this bouquet. Keep turning your vase and filling in gaps, always staying within the original lines created by your foliage and line flowers.

6 Cut your flowers to different lengths and insert them at different levels. Notice how I've added the statice throughout the design, after breaking them apart from the main stem. Don't forget to clean off the lower leaves.

tip
-To get your vases sparkling clean, use a couple of teaspoons of bleach or dishwasher detergent, fill with hot water and soak for a few hours.

8 Last step is the filler material, in this case Queen Anne's lace. I also added a couple of stems of sword fern and jasmine from my yard.

floral foam

Let's combine floral foam with an inexpensive basket and transform a store-bought bouquet into a stunning arrangement that you would be proud to deliver to a friend in the hospital, as a birthday gift or just to say "I care about you."

1 Separate your bouquet into your layers (remember The Basics?) You're probably going to need to add some greens from your yard. Pull apart the multiple stemmed flowers such as chrysanthemums, carnations and statice, creating many more flowers to work with.

2 Tape floral foam into a liner that fits your basket. Here I've cut down a distilled water bottle. You can use any type of container that will hold water. Be sure to soak your foam, leave one inch above the top of the basket and trim the edges.

3 Insert your foliage first. I added more greens from my yard. Snip your ends to a nice point and trim off any nubs. These leave gaps in the foam and cause your stems to fall out. Point your stems to the imaginary X in the center of your foam. Use leaf shine or rub the leaves on your jeans to make them shiny.

Every store-bought bouquet is different, but I know that you can apply these guidelines and create a beautiful design, no matter what you purchase.

4 I've used solidaster as my line flowers, although it can also be used as filler. Notice how it defines the shape of the arrangement.

5 Now add your mass flowers. This bouquet included yellow carnations and deep pink chrysanthemums. Keep turning your basket, filling in gaps, always pointing toward the imaginary X. Notice how the flowers are at different heights and levels

6 Time for your focal flowers. Sunny gerbera daisies really draw your attention to this arrangement. You might be able to see a couple of sunflowers, but they aren't fully opened.

tips

-A basket of fresh flowers brings a smile to anyone's face. Can you think of someone who could use a smile?

And what fun you will have bringing it to them!

7 Finally, for filler I've added Queen Anne's lace, statice and a bit of curly willow, giving the arrangement added texture and interest. A simple bow accents the pink tones of the mums and adds a final, festive touch.

simple centerpiece

Dress up your dinner table with this easy, inexpensive centerpiece. All you need is a low tray or container. How about that plastic tray from your frozen lunch or a styrofoam meat tray?

1 Soak your floral foam until it's really heavy. Cut it to fit your container, leaving about one inch above the surface. I secured mine with florist's tape, but this isn't necessary if you're careful when you move it.

2 First insert your greens to almost cover the floral foam. I added pitisporum and a little eucalyptus from my yard. Camelia would work well too. Insert stems toward an imaginary X in the center. Turn your tray often and create a dome shape.

3 Next add your line flowers. There may not be many, as was the case with this bouquet, but it really doesn't matter that much, as long as you're following some sort of pattern.

Although mixed bouquets vary when it comes to size, color and mixture of flowers, you can almost always apply these guidelines. And you'll need to add extra greens.

4 Mass flowers are next. These daisy mums were cut from their original "mother" stems. You should do this with almost all multi-stemmed flowers like carnations and statice.

Finish by adding your focal
flowers and filler material.
Looks professional, but you
did it yourself!

hat's *off!*

Wouldn't this make a great centerpiece for your next ladies' club gathering? It was made from a grocery store bouquet. But you could use any color straw or other type of hat and a bouquet of your choice.

1 Separate your foliage and flowers by types as noted in the previous lessons. Place pre-soaked floral foam in a plastic liner that fits your opening.

2 This particular bouquet contained very little foliage, so I cut some myrtle from my yard. I inserted it to form sort of a crescent shape.

3 Camellia is used as round foliage to soften the design and cover the foam. I always like to spray my foliage with leaf shine before adding the flowers.

Next time you buy that grocery store bouquet, get a little creative with your container. Have any hats in your closet?

4 I used two gladiolas for my line flowers then added the chrysanthemums and carnations at various levels. Remember to remove them from the main stems.

5 Focal flowers are next, some toward the base and others a bit higher while still maintaining our crescent shape.

tip

-Always remember to clean your stems of leaves and nubs and snip them at an angle to form a point. Then insert them toward the imaginary X.

6 Purple Queen Anne's lace, statice and wax flower act as filler material. I added a couple of red carnations as well to round it out. And of course, the Purple Plume is a must!

sweet tooth

This is one of my favorite designs. The jelly beans are such a surprise when used with flowers. You can combine almost any type of flowers, including an inexpensive, grocery store bouquet. Just make sure the colors mimic the jelly beans.

1 A small glass tumbler containing pre-soaked floral foam is inserted into a larger cube vase. You could use any clear glass, outer container. Note the foam extending above the top.

2 Fill in the gap with jelly beans. It doesn't take many and you can find inexpensive candy at your discount department store.

3 Add a few greens of your choice. I used salal and leather leaf fern, but if you have enough flowers, you don't need much.

What a fun gift this makes for just about any occasion. And what about using several as centerpieces for a teenager's party?

Simply insert assorted
flowers throughout,
but make sure the candy
is clearly visible.

winter sunshine

F lower selections are pretty limited in the winter months. But you can still find colorful grocery store bouquets like this one to add a splash of summer to your day.

1 Don't have a vase handy? I used a pickle jar! Soak it to remove the label, add water and tape a grid across the top. Jars make wonderful flower vessels. Grouping different types and sizes creates a casual, country look.

2 This bouquet contained more greens than most. I started with salal, pointing the stems toward the center and fanning out the leaves.

3 Next I added the silvery green eucalyptus. You need to work with it to get it evenly dispersed. It just takes a little practice. And if your bouquet didn't provide a lot of greens, look in your yard.

I hope you're getting the idea that grocery store flowers can be transformed into a beautiful, professional looking arrangement with a little time and effort.

4 To act as my line flower, I used all of the white carnations to form a triangle. Remember, you need to cut some of them from the main stem.

5 The same is true for the golden chrysanthemums. Notice how they are cut to different lengths, but remain within the triangle. Don't forget to remove all leaves below the water's surface.

6 You can barely see the three stems of white alstromeria, but they're there. Just look for gaps and use the remaining flowers to fill them.

7 Usually I throw away the colorful paper collar they put around the bouquets, but not this time! I gathered it up around the jar and secured it with a rubber band.

tip

-Tie a ribbon in a contrasting color or a few strands of raffia around the neck for a more finished look. If you don't want to use the paper collar to disguise the pickle jar and hide the stems, what about a piece of burlap, denim or other fabric? Yellow and white polka dots would be fun.

don't eat the daisies

This is such a clean, fresh bouquet. It reminds me of white sheets blowing in the summer breeze on an outdoor clothesline. And the fun part is when everyone tries to guess what you did with the stems.

1 Put a tiny bit of water in a ginger vase, then add a sprig of camellia and a cut lime or lemon. I used a large Lomey pedestal, which can be purchased from a floral supply store.

2 I used a few stems of leather leaf fern, but you can certainly substitute another type of foliage, like ruscus, salal or camellia.

3 Once you have separated your individual mums from the main stem, start inserting them in a dome shaped fashion. Keep turning your vase to ensure an even distribution. As a reminder, a kitchen cabinet turntable like those used for spices makes this part of the job a lot easier.

This simple design is made up of a couple of bunches of daisy chrysanthemums, a little solidaster, and minimal greens.

4 Just keep filling in with mums all around, keeping the design tight and uniform. And don't forget to point all of your stems toward the imaginary X in the center.

tips

If you have trouble with this "invisible stem" technique, you can always use a solid container, say an urn or opaque compote type vase. That way your foam can be placed directly into the container or in another container that fits into the urn. Since these vessels aren't clear, you don't have to worry about the mechanics showing. Just make sure that your foam extends at least an inch above the top.

5 The solidaster gives the arrangement a little "fluff" and accents the colors of the flowers' centers.

garden party

I found watering cans like this one in several different colors at the discount department store, but the orange was my favorite. These would make lovely, innovative centerpieces for your next garden party or bridal shower!

1 I used the taped grid method here, but you could also fill the opening with pre-soaked floral foam.

2 A single hydrangea fills up a lot of space and the lime green looks great with the orange.

3 Next I inserted three pin cushion dahlias in the same orange tone as the watering can.

Keep in mind, this is just one design idea. You could use dozens of different types of flowers, but I wanted to show you how to turn a $5.00 watering can into an eye catching floral container. Be sure yours is watertight. If it's not, you'll need to add a liner or seal the joint with hot glue.

To complete the design, I used a few fragrant roses, a snip of kangaroo paw from my yard and a very twisted kiwi vine.

Tulip

27

can can

Sometimes you can't find the right container for your arrangement. How about making one from your recyclables? These were made using three sizes of tin cans and some old wallpaper.

1 If you don't have any wallpaper lying around, you can always buy a single roll at your home improvement store. You could also use contact paper or heavy wrapping paper. Find a print or texture you like. How many of you remember grass cloth? I just put it in my bathroom!

2 First tape your grids, then measure and cut a piece of the wallpaper to fit each can. Attach the paper to the can using spray adhesive.

This lesson was simple, but it shows you how you can customize a container to compliment a room or it's surroundings. This grouping would look fantastic on your dinner or patio table or a piece of furniture that needs a little pizazz.

Wouldn't this make a fun project to do with your kids? Let them give a "can" of flowers to a favorite teacher, who could use it as a pencil holder when the flowers are past their prime.

3 I added a few stems of magnolia, but you could use any foliage you like. Be sure it's clean; spray it with leaf shine if you can.

Notice how I put 3 gerbera daisies in the large can, 2 in the medium size, and 1 in the smallest can. Of course you could use chrysanthemums, sunflowers or dahlias, too! Cover any visible mechanics (the tape) with moss.

popcorn and a movie

Movie cards are so popular these days and they make a great gift. But instead of handing someone a 3 x 5 card, why not make yours stand out from all the rest?

1 Pop a bunch of air-popped corn or microwave unbuttered popcorn. Cut a clear, 2 liter soda bottle to about the same height as your outer container.

2 Place the soda bottle inside of your outer container and add the popcorn between the two. Push the top of the soda bottle toward the center to make room for the popcorn. Once your popcorn is almost to the top, carefully add water to the soda bottle. You don't want to get any of the popcorn wet. Tape the grid across the outer container.

3 Two stems of blue hydrangea quickly set the stage. Any color will work or you could use several other flowers such as sunflowers, pom pom mums, agapantha, peonies...just make sure you can see the popcorn.

Even without the movie card, this design provides a fun centerpiece or gift.

4 A single, flame colored dahlia vividly illustrates why blue and orange are considered complimentary colors. The ivy isn't necessary, but I thought it added a little more dimension.

Height and balance are achieved with a stem of creamy stock and a curved kiwi branch, to which I've attached the movie card.

gorgeous gerberas

This is a simple, yet elegant design – a basic container, magnolia leaves, gerbera daisies, curly willow and bunny tail. Place it on a coffee or end table and enjoy!

1 Most metal containers are not water tight so you need to put your floral foam in a liner or recyclable plastic tub. Let it extend about an inch above the top.

2 You get a lot of mileage out of a few magnolia tree stems. Make sure they're clean and shiny. Leaf shine is almost a must.

3 Notice how the gerberas are cut to different lengths throughout. Pluck the petals off of a couple of them as I did here. You could also use chrysanthemums in this design.

You can find interesting and inexpensive containers like this one at inventory clearance stores, second hand shops and yard sales. Use moss to cover any visible foam.

A few stems of bunny tail act as filler. You may have something else in your yard that you could use. Once again, curly willow gives the arrangement that certain pizzazz.

wine is for drinking

I received a fantastic bottle of wine in this gift box. Of course, I drank the wine, but what to do with the box??? Why not turn it into a "vase", using a few flowers and filler from my garden.

1 Tape a grid across an ordinary water glass and place it inside your wine box. You don't need to fill it with water. Just make sure your flowers can drink.

2 All that I used here was a single blush dahlia and sapphire hydrangea. You want your flowers to compliment the colors in your wine box.

3 Next I added a couple of plumes from the many purple fountain grass plants in my yard and one stem of a wheat colored grass to pick up that same tone in the box.

You can find so many sturdy gift boxes in all shapes and sizes. Add a waterproof liner or insert and you have a unique and creative flower container!

The black dahlia stems give the design another dimension and continue the deep tones in the wine box. The raffia used to tie the "x" repeats the wheat color.

floral styrofoam

Using a styrofoam deli tray as a base, this stunning centerpiece was created with a few cuttings of yard foliage, three stems of stock, six white roses and three stems of Asiatic lilies, punctuated with lime green kermit mums.

1

1 Soak one block of floral foam and cut it to fit into your tray, trimming the sharp edges. Of course, you could use any type of low, water-tight container. I just like to show you what you can do with free recyclables.

2

2 Fruitless plum trees offer rich foliage in various tones ranging from merlot to chocolate. Remember, foliage doesn't always have to be green!

3 I added a few stems of camellia and lime green cuttings from a tree (type unknown) that had wispy filler material already attached! Remember to snip your ends to a nice point and trim off any nubs. Point your stems toward the imaginary X in the center of your foam. If you have leaf shine, spray your foliage.

3

Once you start working with floral foam, you'll get hooked. It allows you to do so many things with flowers that you can't do with vases.

4 Three stems of spicy, white stock help define the triangular shape of the design. It's fragrance is divine!

4

5   Mass flowers consisted simply of six or seven white roses. Remove any cracked or discolored guard petals. Keep turning your design, filling in gaps, always pointing toward the imaginary X.

6   Dramatic white lilies star as our focal flowers. I like to include the buds for the added texture and color. Notice how they reflect the lime green kermit mums. The chocolate brown anthers accent the plum tree foliage and wispy filler.

pasta party

Combine three floral ingredients with two containers, add a bag of spaghetti and enjoy! Wouldn't this look great as a buffet centerpiece for a casual pasta party?

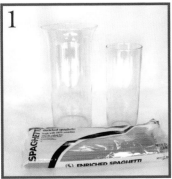

1 You'll need two tall containers. The inner container should fit inside the clear glass outer container with about 1/4 inch gap in between. Maybe use a tall drinking glass for your inner container. It doesn't have to be clear.

2 Place the smaller container inside of the larger one. Drop spaghetti in all around the edge until the inner container is completely hidden.

What are you going to say when your guests ask, "How did you do that?"
What fun you'll have making them guess!

3 I'm using eucalyptus seeds here without the leaves. But you could substitute with any type of "flowy" foliage. I just inserted it into the inner container, to which I've added water, and it becomes a framework for the remaining ingredients. Depending on what you're using, you may want to go with the taped grid method.

Just two or three stems of magnolia foliage create a bold background for five glorious sunflowers. Insert the magnolia first, then add the sunflowers. Two curly willow stems give the arrangement a touch of added rhythm.

roses & pomegranates

This arrangement takes about 2 dozen roses and 5 or 6 pomegranates. Imagine it as the focal point for your next dinner party. If you have several tables, you could make smaller ones for very little cost. The technique is quite simple.

1 Your everyday dinner plate can be used as the base for this beautiful centerpiece. One block of floral foam is soaked, split and arranged on the plate. I taped mine with florist's tape, but you could use cellophane tape, too.

2 Begin to create the shape of your design with your foliage. I used cotinus (smoke bush) because I was going for an autumnal look. Fruitless plum leaves are similar in color and could be used. Eucalyptus, camellia, salal, pitisporum or any other round foliage would work, too.

3 Next, I added Safari Sunset (leucodendron). Most of you won't have this, so don't worry about it. Just add a little more foliage. You can mix your round foliage if you want.

Although I used pomegranates with roses, you could substitute apples, pears, limes, oranges...it depends on the flowers you use.

4 Next start adding your roses in groups of three. You really could use just about any flowers in this arrangement. Chrysanthemums would work well. Notice how we're creating a round, dome shape.

5

5 Continue to fill in with flowers. You don't have to follow the same color pattern I did. Use your imagination and have fun!

tips

-You want all of your colors to blend.

-Notice how the roses are clumped by color rather than "dotted". This technique offers mini focal points throughout the arrangement.

6 Finally, I added the pomegranates. Just impale them with a portion of a bamboo skewer and insert into the floral foam. Very simple! A little orange wax flower provides additional texture, but I won't tell if you don't use it!

6

fit for a queen

Why not give your next formal dinner party a touch of elegance with a beautiful centerpiece like this one. Your guests will think you called the florist, but you can say, "I made it myself".

1 I used a block of floral foam inside of a frozen food tray. Remember how you created the shape of your design in the vased arrangement in Chapter 2? Now we're going to do it with floral foam.

2 After defining the size and shape of the arrangement with eucalyptus (you can use any other line foliage), I filled in with leather leaf fern.

3 Continue the triangular shape with line flowers like these lime green bells of Ireland along with fuchsia and lilac stock.

4 Notice how iris can act as line flowers or mass flowers, depending on their stage of bloom.

5 The pink and white rose buds look so pretty with the lavender and green tones. Cut them to various lengths and insert throughout the design.

tip

Remember, you can use your own choice of flowers. The goal here is to teach you to create a long centerpiece with floral foam and your recyclables using the layer technique.

6 Seashell pink lilies provide a lovely focal point and just a touch of pink wax flower is used as filler. You don't need the taper candle, but it will provide your dinner table with such a warm glow.

Floating flowers have always been a popular centerpiece. Here are a few ideas that are quite inexpensive and take very little time to create. But the color combinations provide a dazzling display as a focal point for your guest tables.

sweet & simple centerpieces

1 This one uses two stems of Bells of Ireland twisted around the bottom of a bowl vase and a couple of snips from a blue hydrangea. Royal or navy linens would create a stunning backdrop.

2 A column candle is surrounded by Bells of Ireland florets and four or five bubble gum dahlias. Picture this on a pink table cloth with a white overlay.

3 Same idea, but using fewer Bell florets with golden roses. Yummy on a mint linen. Golden yellow napkins would compliment the roses.

4

4 For an afternoon event, you can omit the candle. Here I've randomly twisted two stems of Bells of Ireland and dotted them with apricot roses. This is one of my favorite color combinations.

If you're planning a large event on a small budget, centerpieces like these offer maximum impact at a minimal cost. And any member of your decorating committee can do them!

tips

-Lower bowls can certainly be used with floating flowers and petals. And you may want to add river stones or glass beads.

-Sometimes all you need is one large floating flower, such as a magnificent magnolia or peony.

5

5 For a taller look, use a hurricane vase and candle. Float some florets around the sides and twist a stem around the top to create a beautiful, lime green crown. Scatter a few florets on the table. They'll last throughout the party.

6 A single pink dahlia rests atop sapphire hydrangea petals and repeats itself just outside this simple, cylindrical container. Pink and blue...maybe a baby shower?

6

simple topiary

What a charming centerpiece this makes for just about any celebration, birthday party, garden party, shower, even a wedding! It's simple and inexpensive.

1 The container holding my pre-soaked floral foam was purchased from the dollar store. I gathered a few stems of blue hydrangea with a couple of apricot roses and secured them with rubber bands.

2 Cut your stems to an even length that balances with the height of your container. Then simply insert the bunch into the foam.

3 Cover the foam with your choice of greens. I used variegated ivy because I liked the way it spills over the sides and almost repeats the shape of the flower bunch.

Of all of the elements that impact a design, color is probably one of the most important. The complimentary colors of vibrant orange and deep, lavender blue really make this arrangement stand out in a crowd. And note how the container picks up the soft greens in a small section of the hydrangea.

Fill in the base with a few hydrangea stems and roses. Make a festive bow with coordinating wired ribbon.

instant

All of these arrangements use a single type of flower. They're quick and easy to make, yet create a beautiful focal point for the table.

centerpieces

1 Two aspidistra leaves are curled inside this simple glass vase, to which I've added a small amount of water. Float one fully opened lily and add two or three more cut stems. This creates an elegant and stately arrangement for a single table or an entire banquet room. Lilies come in so many colors, too!

2 Again, a couple of aspidistra leaves line the bottom of this rose bowl. You could also use philodendron, anthurium or other large leaves. Gently massage the calla lily stems so they bend and randomly insert them into the bowl. The lemon was added just for fun.

3 To make this dainty design, gather about eight tulips and secure them with a rubber band. Then wrap a tulip leaf around the bundle and fasten with a straight pin. Twisted curly willow inside the cube vase gives the arrangement rhythm and added interest, along with a couple of twigs extending outside the vase.

4 Mason jars filled with alstromeria and tied with raffia make wonderful centerpieces for a casual affair. You could use one per table or group them like this.

tip

-All of these flowers come in a rainbow of colors. Coordinate them with your linens and/or dishes whenever possible.

All of these designs are quick, easy and inexpensive!

5 A few seashells on a bed of sand pick up the pink tones in these gorgeous lilies. They are on a single stem inserted into a water pick.

6 Using the taped grid method, I grouped coral alstromeria with gerbera daisy centers (note the partially de-petaled gerb outside the vase). A swirl of flax leaves disguises the stems and provides added interest and rhythm.

49

baby bucket

Perfect for a baby shower centerpiece, this design uses dollar store finds and a variety of flowers in pastel tones suitable for any tiny gender.

1 A dollar bucket acts as our pedestal. I used a liner from the hardware store into which I added floral foam. Be sure to secure it with tape.

2 Cover the foam with round foliage of your choice. I used variegated ivy. The blocks are glued together and nestled in the greens along with the duckies, all of which cost $1.00.

I know you probably won't have access to all of the flowers I used, but I wanted you to see how, with a little imagination, you can create a centerpiece for any celebration at a minimal cost.

3 Creamy stock and lilac delphinium define the line of our design. You don't necessarily need any line flowers. A round, dome shape would look great, too. But a little added dimension almost never hurts.

4 Note the rhythm created by the lime green bells of Ireland and three stems of ivy. One pink dahlia and a sapphire hydrangea are the first of our mass flowers.

Various types of pastel flowers are added throughout this arrangement. There really are no focal flowers. Your attention is drawn to the blocks and duckies.

aloha!

This is a pretty economical centerpiece for your Hawaiian luau, as it uses a lot of greens and very few flowers.

1 These miniature tiki torches were around $5.00 at the craft store. I used a hammer to detach the base, which you don't need. A couple of pounds and it came right off.

2 The tiki torch is then inserted into pre-soaked floral foam. I used a florist's bowl, but note that you could also use a frozen food tray or bowl instead. Recycle!

3 To make an aspidistra curl, cut the stem to a sharp point. Bend the other end over and pierce it with the stem. You may need to give it a little help with the point of a knife.

4 The heaviness of the aspidistra leaves help to balance the weight of the torch. A single xanadu leaf offers rhythm and shape variation.

5

5 My remaining greens consisted of salal and leather leaf fern. Next I added a single lily stem, including the buds, and a yummy, yellow pincushion protea.

tip

-If you have several tables at your party, you may want to vary the colors and make each centerpiece a little different. Remember, lilies and alstromeria come in a rainbow of lush, tropical colors.

6   The mango color is introduced with a couple of stems of alstromeria. That's all you really need.

6

the Mason jar

How many of us have spent long, hot summer hours canning vegetables? Forget about it! Put those mason jars to a much better use and don't sweat in the process. This is so quick and simple! Wouldn't these make cute centerpieces at your next party, using different types of flowers in each one? What a great way to use home-grown flowers!

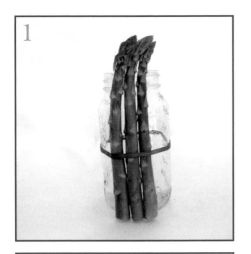

1 You'll need about a pound and a half of asparagus to fit around the average Mason jar. Cut them at equal lengths and insert into a rubber band around the middle of the jar.

2 When the jar is concealed, tie raffia around the rubber band to hide it. You could also use ribbon. Play around!

Think of what else you could use around the jar: What about carrots, celery sticks, rhubarb, leeks, or even thick flower stems? A bunch of alstromeria would look great enclosed by their own stems. Cinnamon sticks or candy canes during the holidays. Need a cute gift for a teacher? Why not put pencils around the jar?

The possibilities are endless!

Now simply add your flowers! I just inserted a bunch of ranunculas tied with a rubber band. But you could use almost any flower. Add foliage if you want.

split pea soup

Using interesting inserts and the container inside a container technique, you can create some really fun designs.

1 Tape a grid across your inner container like this tin can. Don't add water to it until after you've inserted the peas. Aren't recyclables the best!

2 Place your inner container inside a larger, clear container like this craft store cylinder. Then add your rows of peas. You will probably spill a few – it's inevitable.

3 Continue adding layers until you get to the top. If peas spill into the inner container, fish then out with a piece of cellophane tape before adding water.

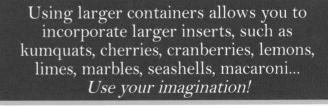

Using larger containers allows you to incorporate larger inserts, such as kumquats, cherries, cranberries, lemons, limes, marbles, seashells, macaroni... *Use your imagination!*

4 I used a grocery store bouquet but you could use garden flowers. This one included a generous amount of salal, one of my favorite greens.

5 I cut apart the multi-stemmed, white carnations in the bouquet and inserted them throughout the vase, creating a dome shape. Remember to point your stems toward the center.

6 These perky yellow daisy mums were also separated from the main stem before adding them to the arrangement. Keep turning your vase and filling in gaps.

7

O nce you get the hang of adding inserts, this is a pretty fast and easy arrangement to create. It would make a lively centerpiece for your next party.

What fun you can have coming up with interesting inserts and pairing them with your flowers!

7 Finally, I added the three stems of white alstromeria and the carnation buds. Simple, quick, but so pretty!

pincushions & artichokes

Ok, so there's only one artichoke flanked by two luscious pincushion protea, one orange and one yellow. Four sunny tulips reflecting both those colors, combined with three novelty leucodendron, three aspidistra leaves, a bit of bear grass and a twist of kiwi vine create this artful display.

tips

Have fun substituting flowers in this design.

-with the artichoke as the focal point, you could use roses in place of the leucodendron, and large pods or pom pom mums in place of the protea.

Use your imagination!

1 Twist a handful of bear grass around a cylinder, then add an aspidistra leaf to hide the floral foam. Cut your soaked foam to fit, level with the top and place it inside the vase.

2 To create an aspidistra curl, cut the stem to a sharp point. Fold the opposite end under about an inch. Bring the stem end around and pierce the folded end. If piercing is difficult, put a tiny slice through the fold with the tip of a sharp knife.

3 Place the artichoke in front and use two aspidistra curls as a backdrop. If your artichoke stem is too short, you can use two pieces of a bamboo skewer to insert it into the foam.

The order in which you add the remaining ingredients really doesn't matter; maybe work backwards, adding the two protea, then the leucodendron, next the tulips and finally the kiwi.

citrus punch

Get your daily requirement of vitamin C with this arrangement! But where did the stems go? I used a clear glass hurricane container, a plastic liner, floral foam, sunflowers, lilies, pincushion protea, kiwi vine, curly willow and citrus fruit to create this summery design.

1 Twist the kiwi vine in your hand and then work it into the vase. If you don't have kiwi, you can use any flexible material like curly willow. Or try cuttings from your maple or other trees. Next add your citrus. Think of what else you can use...apples, pomegranates.

2 A plastic liner from the hardware store fits perfectly into the vase opening. Soak your floral foam and cut it to fit the liner, leaving about an inch above the top. Put a couple of pieces of tape across the top to keep everything in place.

3 Start with your greens. I used round foliage here (camellia) and made sure it draped over the sides to hide the mechanics.

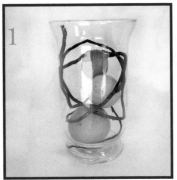

4 Start adding your flowers, pointing toward an imaginary X in the center and making sure there are no nubs on the stems. The "green" sunflower is actually a yellow sunflower with the petals pulled off.

A couple of these on a buffet table look gorgeous, but take up little space, thus leaving room for the food! And they're not too tall to act as guest table centerpieces. You could even add a few random oranges, lemons and limes scattered on the table for added zest!

One or two Asiatic lily stems add height to the arrangement and a couple of clippings of curly willow give it rhythm.

61

welcome to the neighborhood

This cheery arrangement, designed inside of a colander, offers a warm welcome to a new neighbor, or creates a festive, yet practical gift for anyone who loves to cook.

1 I found this gleaming, red colander at an inventory clearance store for less than eight dollars. A block of pre-soaked floral foam has been cut down slightly and taped into a plastic liner. Since the liner won't show, you can use just about any type of water tight container...maybe a margarine tub or disposable food storage container. Make sure the foam is about one inch taller than the colander.

2 Add your greens first. I used variegated bush ivy, but just about any type of foliage should work. You may want to use salal, camellia, pitsporum or even a mixture. Use it to form a dome shape, pointing each stem toward that imaginary X in the center. Don't forget to spray your foliage with leaf shine.

3 To give the design a touch of added color, I included a few stems of cotinus, also known as "smoke tree". An alternative would be fruitless plum. Or just use ivy!

4 The scarlet dahlias pick up the color of the colander. Red roses, gerbera daisies or Red Rover chrysanthemums would also work. The object is to have your flowers compliment your container.

5 Three golden sunflowers provide a nice contrast to the red tones, and the dark centers pick up the color of the cotinus. Colorful gerbera daisies would also work well.

tip

You don't need the dish towel, but it was only a dollar! I couldn't resist. This could also be used as a table centerpiece for a casual dinner party.

6 I finished this design with a few burgundy colored leucodendron (safari sunset), a couple of stems of flaming crocosmia and you can barely see two or three fuzzy coneflowers (which are actually de-petaled echinacea flowers). Curly willow provides just a hint of rhythm.

63

coffee anyone?

One of my favorite parts of this arrangement is the fact that the beautiful, rhythmic maple twigs were free! I saved them when I did my annual pruning. What can you be saving that until now you considered rubbish?

1 This is so easy! I bought the larger glass cylinder from my craft store. The smaller container is just an old glass tumbler. See if your favorite coffee house has any beans they can't use for whatever reason. Otherwise, get the least expensive bag you can find.

This is another, simple yet eye-catching design that anyone can do! And what makes it even more fun? You get a whiff of coffee every time you go near it! Who doesn't like that?

2 Begin by taping a grid across your tumbler or whatever small container you're using, maybe a margarine tub or yogurt container. Place it inside the cylinder and pour coffee beans between the two.

Now insert any color of Asiatic lily, although I love the contrast of the orange and brown. What makes this work so well is how the coffee beans mimic the color of the rich brown lily anthers. The maple twigs add yet another element of rhythm, while repeating the deep, cappuccino tones.

boxed beauties

Almost anything can be used to hold flowers! This pavé design is such an innovative way to present a "bouquet" of flowers to a friend, even a guy. It also makes a very creative centerpiece.

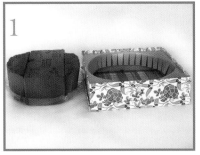

1 I saw this gift box on sale at the craft store and couldn't resist. A plastic liner from the hardware store fit perfectly. It took about 1 ½ blocks of floral foam cut level with the box.

4 Rows of hot pink and crimson roses continue to add to our masterpiece. Note that we're using the complimentary colors of red and green.

2 Once again, remember to select flowers that compliment the color of your container. These dahlias do the trick! Even the shape is similar to the flowers on the box. Start in the center of your foam and work your way out.

3 Tiny green apples and bells of Ireland florets pick up the lime green tones. I used bamboo skewers to insert the apples.

Pavé designs are a lot of fun and fairly easy to do. And there are so many ways to create them, not only using florals, but all kinds of nature's wonders. As always, use your imagination and think outside the box. Well, except in this case!

The last of the exposed floral foam is covered with white roses, again coordinating with the colors in the box.

ouch! feel better

Cotton balls, band-aids and Q-tips convey your sincere wish that the recipient of this thoughtful gift will feel better soon.

1 Two bags of cotton balls, band-aids, Q-tips, a large vase and a smaller one comprise the mechanics. Use the container inside a container technique... water inside the inner container with your taped grid.

2 Place the smaller container inside the larger one and stuff the gaps with cotton balls and Q-tips. Then stick band-aids randomly around the outside of the large vase. Get the box of assorted sizes if possible.

3 Make a cozy little bed of greens for your flowers in the inner container. I started with leather leaf fern but, as always, you can substitute with ruscus, huckleberry, myrtle or other line foliage. Remember to point your stems toward the imaginary X in the center.

You can use smaller containers if you prefer and many other types of flowers. The main thing is to be able to see all the "doctor stuff".

4 Here I've used seeded eucalyptus for my round foliage because I like the way it drapes over the sides. Plus, the seeds provide additional texture and color. You could also use salal, camellia, ivy, pitisporum or other round foliage.

5 Three stems of blue delphinium will provide a nice contrast to the apricot roses. Most of you probably know that blue and orange are complimentary colors. You can go with your own colors, but I liked the way the roses reflected the color of the band-aids.

I seriously doubt you could order an arrangement like this from a florist. If the patient is in the hospital, can you imagine the comments it will evoke from the staff?

Just one more way to have fun with flowers!

6 Eight yummy roses and a few pincushion dahlias toward the base complete this arrangement. I chose not to use filler with this one, as it didn't seem to need it. Remember, you can use just about any type of flowers. The attraction of this design is in the mechanics. Use your imagination.

comical kitty

Colorful coffee mugs make great, inexpensive gifts. But alone, they don't seem like enough. For a few dollars more and a little bit of your time, you have a custom gift that will generate smile after smile.

1 Again, an inventory clearance store was brimming with a huge variety of whimsical mugs of all shapes and sizes. I really had trouble choosing, but I was drawn to the brilliant colors of this one, depicting Queen of the Cats. Of course, for only $4.99, I could have bought several. Cutting the pre-soaked floral foam to fit was a little tricky, but I know you can do it. Let it rise about an inch above the top.

2 For my greens, I used a few stems of ming fern and a little seeded eucalyptus, forming a triangle to set the size and shape of my design. You're working on such a small scale, I'm sure you can find enough foliage in your yard for this type of arrangement. Remember, don't just focus on bushes and shrubs. Consider tree branches as well. Don't cut young, new foliage as this will not hold up in an arrangement. Older, more established stems are preferable. Be sure they're clean and shiny. Make the ends as "pointy" as possible and direct them toward the imaginary X in the center.

3 As always, you want your flowers to compliment your container. You don't need very many. You could probably get a small, inexpensive, mixed bouquet and have enough flowers to create a beautiful design. Here I used about four dahlias and a single sunflower. Notice how the colors blend so well with those in the mug, right down to the sunflower's center reflecting the black tones on the handle, cat and base design. Have your mug with you as you select your flowers.

Imagine giving a fun and festive gift like this to a co-worker for a birthday, promotion or other special occasion. You'll be the talk of the office (but in a good way)!

The single stem of kangaroo paw came from my backyard. It worked so well with the lemon-lime tones in the mug, that I just had to use it. And it seems you can't go wrong with a little curly willow in almost any arrangement. If you don't have any, try a few twigs from another type of tree, such as birch or maple. Play around and see what you can come up with. If you chose a store bought bouquet that contained lily or bear grass, you could use that for rhythm. To insert it into the foam, use a wired pick or tape it around a piece of a bamboo skewer.

71

puppy love

Need a quick but impressive gift for a dog lover? Milk bones for puppies surround these vibrant sunflowers, but you could also create this design on a larger scale using "grown up" Milk Bones and taller containers.

1 Let's use our popular container inside a container technique. I used a glass cylinder from my local craft store as my outer container and a glass tumbler inside. A small jelly jar would work too. Add water to the inner container and make a grid across the top. And don't forget to buy the Milk Bones for puppies.

3 This design is so easy! Add a few stems of your greens. I used variegated bush ivy, but as always, you can substitute, as long as it is in proportion to your container. Just make a little nest for your flowers.

2 Place the small container inside the larger one and insert the dog biscuits around the sides between the two. Start with a row at the bottom all around before going to the top. This helps position the small container so that the biscuits don't end up pushing it to one side. You may want to temporarily cover the inner container with a lid so that none of the Milk Bone spills into the water. If this happens, be sure to remove them.

Wouldn't it be fun to give this to a friend to welcome the arrival of a new puppy into their family? The "parents" get to enjoy the flowers and when they expire (the flowers, not the parents), Max will get to munch on the cookies!

72

Four or five sunflowers, a few scabiosa pods and two sunflower stems complete this adorable arrangement. You may want to use gerbera daisies, chrysanthemums, cosmos or even a mixed assortment. But the simpler you keep it, the more you notice the doggy treats.

happy birthday to you!

This colorful "Happy Birthday" gift box was on sale at a craft store for less than three dollars. A few daisy mums, carnations, solidaster and curling ribbon turn it into a customized gift that ends up costing about a fourth of what it would if you didn't make it yourself.

1 This used cheese container makes the perfect liner for our gift box. I can't stress enough the value in having a generous supply of plastic recyclables on hand in various shapes and sizes. I call it "green flower arranging"! Cut pre-soaked floral foam to fit and let it extend about an inch above the top of the box.

3 Once you've removed your daisies from the main stems, cut them and insert them into the foam, turning the box, filling in the gaps, pointing the stems toward the X and creating a dome. Always be conscious of how your flowers and foliage blend with your containers.

2 Make a cozy little bed of greens for your flowers. I used leather leaf fern and pitisporum. You can use just about any type of foliage, but you don't want to hide the box. Remember to point your stems toward the imaginary X in the center and create a dome shape. Spray your greens with leaf shine if possible. Clean, shiny leaves look so much more professional.

4 You really don't even need the two-tone carnations, but I had them and they do give another layer of texture. But if you just want to use daisy mums, that's perfectly fine. In fact, I kept going back and forth on which I liked better - with or without the carnations.

tip

I love this arrangement. And there are so many designs and colors of gift boxes available that it's easy to find one that will go with just about any type and color of flowers. And they're so inexpensive! I hope you had as much fun as I did with this little trick.

5 Once again, I've used solidaster as my filler, but you could substitute baby's breath, wax flower, heather or nothing! Filler isn't always needed. But since this is a birthday bouquet, I would encourage you to add the ribbon curls. Choose ribbon colors that blend with the flowers and the gift box.

75

treasure chest

These brilliant protea and leucodendron remind me of precious jewels inside this craft store trinket box. It was on sale for less than six dollars.

1 Using a frozen food tray as my liner, I created my foliage "nest" with linear myrtle, glossy magnolia leaves and seeded eucalyptus. Then I added the colossal, orange banksia. Notice how the magnolia and banksia balance one **another**.

2 One flame colored pincushion protea and one golden protea compliment the banksia in both color and texture.

3 Crimson safari sunset leucodendron extend the line of the design and the smaller, pale yellow leucodendron complete this tropical arrangement. I placed a few twigs across the back for fun.

This design illustrates what you can achieve by thinking outside the box as far as the overall shape and line. Balance is the key.

Using the same foliage as "Treasure Chest", I created an entirely different look with a couple of teddy bear sunflowers, a few sprigs of solidaster and a single, plump artichoke.

...*more* treasure

It's fun to experiment with different materials. Don't just think flowers. Try looking at the produce aisles in a whole new way!

let's color

Wouldn't a favorite grandma or aunt love to get this from your child for their birthday or Mother's Day or just to say "I love you"? This was created with another store-bought bouquet, an inexpensive gift box from my craft store, two sided carpet tape from the hardware store, and a box of 64 crayons.

tips

This entire project probably costs less than $20.00. But look how original it is! You couldn't buy this at your local grocery store or florist shop. And now that you're getting the knack of working with foam and store-bought bouquets, you can put this together in no time.

Visualize the excitement your child will feel as you both (or all, if you have more than one) deliver it to that special person in their lives.

1 Put two rows of carpet tape around the box. Then attach the crayons all the way around. Make sure they go to the bottom. Don't leave the lid on the bottom like I did in this photo.

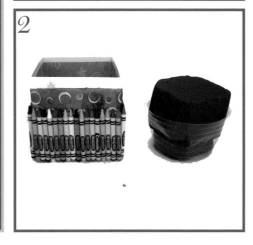

2 I added ribbon around the top, but this isn't necessary if your box is festive enough. Find a liner that fits inside your box. I'm sure you could do better than I did. A large cottage cheese tub is probably just the right height. You want your floral foam to extend above the top of the box about an inch.

Get a bouquet that contains lots of the bright Crayola colors. This one was great because it was mostly gerbera daisies. Remember to strip off the multi-stemmed flowers, such as statice, carnations and chrysanthemums. Just insert the flowers and foliage into your foam, letting some droop over the sides and follow a dome shape. Have your child write a personal note and attach it to a twig.

collage of ideas

These arrangements should get your creative juices flowing. They show you what can be done using just a few flowers in a smart and stylish way.

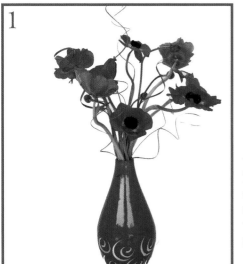

1 Scarlet anemones twirl and dance atop an intriguing vase purchased from an inventory clearance store for about $3.00. Matching the color of your flowers to your vase gives a sophisticated, sleek look.

2 Chocolate cosmos are reflected in the deep brown tones of these beer bottles. I guess beer isn't really considered "sophisticated", but this would be a fun way to jazz up a barbecue or poker party.

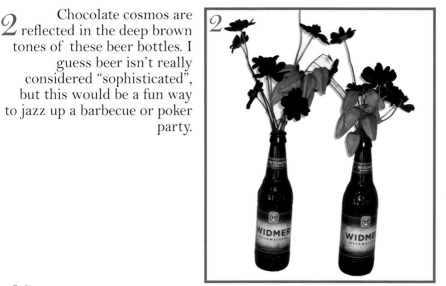

3 You can also match your foliage to the vase, like I did here with a bit of pitisporum and a handful of steel grass tied in the center and placed horizontally across the top.

80

4 Even the smallest of vessels can be used to display miniature bouquets like these royal purple anemones crowned with a golden calla lily.

tips

You don't always need a lot of flowers to brighten up a room or add some color to your environment. Sometimes "simple" is sensational!

5 If you only have a short vase, but you want to have a tall arrangement, you can sometimes extend the height like I did here with a few flax leaves. A very twisted curly willow branch adds dramatic rhythm to what might otherwise be a rather plain design.

6 Three lipstick gerbera daisies are flanked by a bold magnolia leaf, two maple twigs and a sprig of eucalyptus. Attention is demanded by the single flax leaf twisted around this simple, but pleasing design.

smoky *sunset*

This arrangement is a little more complicated than some, but if you follow the steps, you'll do fine. I used aspidistra leaves, several stems of Safari sunset leucodendron, cotinus (smoke tree) and seeded eucalyptus. Only a few dahlias were used to create the richly dramatic design.

1 My container used to hold a rotisserie chicken. The foam extends about an inch above the top. The aspidistra curl was made by cutting the stem to a sharp point, folding the tip of the leaf under and poking the stem through the fold. You may need to help it with a small slit from your knife.

2 Begin to create the shape of your design with the aspidistra leaves. You can do a round design if you prefer it to a crescent.

3 Start filling in with cotinus. A good substitute would be fruitless plum tree cuttings. Note how the crescent shape is being formed.

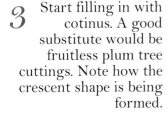

4 I added a little bit of seeded eucalyptus near the base. Then I inserted the leucodendron throughout (see photo #5).

5   It only took four or five stems of coordinating dahlias to give a punch of color. Gerbera daisies, chrysanthemums, lilies and a number of other focal flowers would also make a lovely design. And, of course, you don't have to follow the same color pattern I did. Use your imagination and have fun!

tip

-This makes a beautiful centerpiece, coffee table, or hearth arrangement.

-Experiment with different color "greens". Look around your yard for its hidden treasures!

6   The orange tones were repeated with about seven stems of crocosmia. I like the texture offered by the feathery purple fountain grass from my yard. The cone flowers (echinacea) lend another interesting element, but one of my favorite parts of this design are the two, brown-black dahlia stems.

83

lily basket

Sometimes a single type of flower is all you need to make a dramatic statement, like the luscious lilies in this elegant design.

1 Place a block of pre-soaked floral foam into a liner. A recycled margarine tub would also work well. So that it doesn't show, line the basket with large leaves or even moss.

2 Remember to let your foam extend about an inch above the top so that you can drape your greens down the sides of the basket. I used glossy camellia leaves.

3 Next I added the lilies, including several of the buds. Of course, you could use a different type of flower or even an assortment. Remember to turn your basket and fill in gaps.

tip

-Lily pollen will stain, so you may want to remove the anthers, although I really like the color they provide. If any pollen gets on the petals, a pipe cleaner lifts it off nicely.

I love the way the bunny tail mimics the lily buds and provides additional texture at the same time. Other filler like solidaster or baby's breath could also be used.

dollar store fun

While cruising the dollar store I spotted this adorable, retro telephone along with the camera in the next lesson. Give an arrangement like this one to an office co-worker as a gift or use it as a centerpiece for their going away/retirement party.

1 Split a block of pre-soaked floral foam lengthwise and tape it into a water tight tray like this former edamame container.

2 Dahlia stems fit perfectly into the holes on the bottom of the phone and will be used to stabilize it in the foam.

Themed arrangements are so much fun. You can almost always find a little something that relates to the event or the recipient that really personalizes the design.

3 The only greens I used were variegated ivy, which I sprayed with leaf shine.

4 Three stems of white stock repeat the lighter color in the ivy and act as a backdrop for the phone.

5 Next I "pillowed" four brilliant dahlias across the center. You could use just about any large flower here - gerbera daisies, mums, lilies, sunflowers, etc.

tip

-If your recyclables can be used to hold water or floral foam, don't toss them! I have a box of them in my garage and I seldom have to buy liners or plastic trays from the floral supply store.

6 Fiery crocosmia provide a linear extension, echinacea centers add fuzzy texture and the pencils pull it all together.

say cheese

Although the picture frame says "Happy Birthday", this variation of the previous lesson would also make a great centerpiece for a Bon Voyage party.

1 Start with the same mechanics described in "Dollar Store Fun". I put the camera in the center rather than to the back as I did with the telephone.

tip

-Although similar to the previous lesson, this shows you how a different type of flower with the same foliage creates a completely different look.

2 Next I added a couple of sunflowers and a few stems of smoke bush to mimic the deep tones in the camera.

3 Notice how I inserted the Gold Strike roses into the smoke bush so it looks like they have chocolate leaves.

A few staggered, de-petaled echinacea, chocolate twigs and a photo frame complete this dollar store design.

Happy Birthday!

bashful bouquet

This bountiful bouquet combines several shades of blush pink tones. It's almost monochromatic, except for the creamy whites and lime green. Note how the colors compliment the basket.

1 Baskets make wonderful flower containers, but how do you keep them from leaking? With a liner like this cut down distilled water bottle. A milk carton is another good choice. I used an Exacto knife and it was quite simple.

2 Here I used the clustering technique. Five raspberry calla lilies drape over the side. Clusters of hot pink and white roses are separated by lush green foliage.

3 I like the rhythm created by the three stems of rosey heather. Creamy hypericum buds provide added texture, and pink lilies make a lovely focal flower.

tip

-Clustering your flowers throughout your design provides several, mini focal points. You can cluster by flower type and by color.

For more fullness, I filled in with a little more heather, lilies, hypericum and a few ranunculas. Two stems of bells of Ireland balance out the green tones.

christmas secret

The secret lies in how you got the popcorn and cranberries into the container without getting them wet.

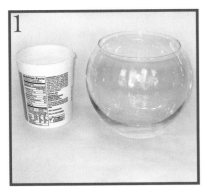

1 Start with a rose bowl and inner container such as a cottage cheese tub. Your inner container should be almost the same height, but not as wide as your bowl.

2 Cut pre-soaked floral foam to fit into the inner container, leaving about an inch above the top. Trim the sharp edges to allow more space for flowers and greens.

3 Combine air-popped popcorn with half a bag of cranberries and fill the gap between the two containers.

Picture this as a beautiful holiday centerpiece or one-of-a-kind hostess gift that will cause everyone to wonder how you did it. And it's quite inexpensive, using only eight roses, home-grown greens, and a few simple ornaments.

4 I used redwood tree clippings from my yard to create a triangular nest for my flowers. You could also use pine or fir. Strip the bottom portion and point them toward the center X.

5 These roses are gorgeous, but you could use another type of flower such as carnations or chrysanthemums. You want them to blend with the berries. You could even use an assortment of flowers, as long as you have some red ones.

6 After removing the "cap" from the red ornaments, I placed a discarded rose stem in the globe and then inserted several into the foam throughout the design.

tips

-A few lime green Kermit mums add a splash of complimentary color.

-A bit of curly willow and a festive red bow complete the package.

index